CINDERELLA

ᐸᴼᴼᐳ HAS ᐸᴼᴼᐳ

CELLULITE

AND OTHER MUSINGS
FROM A LAST WIFE

DONNA ARP WEITZMAN

GREENLEAF
BOOK GROUP PRESS

Published by Greenleaf Book Group Press
Austin, Texas
www.gbgpress.com

Distributed by Greenleaf Book Group

For ordering information or special discounts for bulk purchases, please contact Greenleaf Book Group at PO Box 91869, Austin, TX 78709, 512-891-6100.

Design and composition by Greenleaf Book Group and Debbie Berne
Cover design by Greenleaf Book Group and Debbie Berne

Publisher's Cataloging-in-Publication Data is available.

ISBN: 978-1-62634-209-5

Part of the Tree Neutral® program, which offsets the number of trees consumed in the production and printing of this book by taking proactive steps, such as planting trees in direct proportion to the number of trees used: www.treeneutral.com

TreeNeutral™

Printed in the United States of America on acid-free paper

15 16 17 18 19 20 10 9 8 7 6 5 4 3 2

Second Edition

Other Edition:
eBook ISBN: 978-1-62634-210-1

To my husband, Herb Weitzman. As Herb read each section after I wrote it, he found the humor, as I did, in the musings of a last wife. He stayed by my side as I traversed the precarious path of a Cinderella romance and never wavered in his love and support. Herb is special.

And to my sister, Betty Jean Wilbanks. She knows my every thought and is part of the air I breathe. She rejoices with me, chides me when I'm crazy, supports me when I'm low, brings me back to sanity when I flip out, and always loves me.

My readers, I hope you are as blessed.

CONTENTS

I want to acknowledge my sons, Brandon and Collin, who have lovingly lived with their mom being a Last Wife.

And to my Last Wife friends who have been my inspiration and shared the journeys of Last Wives with me, thank you.

ODE TO A LAST WIFE

Oh, ye to thee
that's number Three.
You are just another
in his she-tree!

Down can be lonely
when your love stalls,
And it hurts when others
rejoice in your fall.

If you think his love
is such a blast,
The day could come
when you won't be his Last!

But being the Last
is much better than zero;
Love can conquer,
and He your hero.

Don't let the numbers
scare you away;
You worry your head
some other day.

Yes, hope springs eternal
and life must go on,
As you get cozy
on your own little throne.

Being Third in a trilogy
Can bring out the best;
You smile like Madonna,
    you pity the rest.

My sisters, be warned
of the ups and the downs.
Being Third in the household
can tarnish the crown.

Keep an eye on his switch-itch,
    the potential's alive;
His next Wife could be
    number four or five.

If He swan dives into
the Next little nest,
You'll move quietly aside
and make room for the rest.

But Tomorrow's the Future,
    and this is Today!
I'm ready, I'm happy,
and I'm here to stay.

PREFACE

I have always thought that books should be about big things, larger than life people, bold actions and ideas. Maybe that is why I have felt a lifelong inadequacy when writing about anything. Who am I to write a book? Nobody would want to read it, and if they did, they'd laugh at me and think, *What a waste of time*!

While writing this book, I realized that I have been consistent throughout my entire life: that is, consistently, desperately lurching for approval. I have never been able to get enough approval, to the point of being angry when I did not get it. Words are inadequate for me to explain what I suffered when easily attained approval turned out to be beyond my grasp during my Cinderella journey. My Prince is good-looking. He is smart and successful. I really want his approval and that of everybody around him. (Oops, there I go again!) The more desperately I lurched, the less I got. Doesn't seem fair, but who said life is fair?

Nevertheless, I hope you'll be "in the moment" with me. Read my musings through the clenched jaw and throbbing headaches I suffered, and you will see a woman of 60 who was furious because she was no one's Princess.

Above all, have hope and humor as you imagine yourself in these circumstances. Take heart, we've all been there at least once. Go back in your mind and revisit your thoughts and actions. Hopefully, you were and are wiser than I am, and handled yourself with much more skill. The good news for me is that I survived, and now I can thrive. But, yikes, I stepped in it often . . . hopefully you can be a better ballerina!

INTRODUCTION

Ah, love. A second chance. Oops, I mean third chance. Fourth? Well, who's counting anyway?

Ah, love. How perfect! All you can think about is having someone to come home to at night. Someone who will wrap his arms around you and protect you from the outside world, singles bars, the boogeyman and crazy people. That special man who will hear your thoughts (after all, you *do* have wonderful thoughts!) and make all your dreams come true.

You can't wait to tell your friends that you have found the One, can you? The world sees you in a different light now. You are headed down the aisle . . .

. . . Or is it a gauntlet?

It is likely that ever since the fateful night your eyes fixated on your Hunk of Burning Love, there have been numerous outbreaks of questions and concerns. Being a Last Wife, you know this is not His first rodeo. As you prepare to saddle up in your vintage Dale Evans fringe and ride off into the sunset with your cowboy, it is wise to know just how close the arrows are that are whizzing next to your scalp. Pull your sombrero closer to your ears, Amiga, this could be a wild ride!

To assume the coveted position of Last Wife, you will experience, at best, a mixed bag of comments with scattered compliments delivered by His menagerie of acquaintances and your well-meaning support groups. But beware, Besotted Beauty, of nefarious jabs piercing your newly formed love handles (acquired during your numerous love trysts). These pricks are likely the diabolical attempts of Camilla-like warfare on unwary Princess Diana—and they can hurt.

Thus, the purpose of this book, Cinderella, is to warn you that you will need your rubber galoshes as you walk in the sun holding his hand. Yes, the perfect day could end in a short, but torrential downpour and a maze of mud holes resembling the Everglades. Whether you choose to gingerly step over or around the sludge, or wade directly through the mire, it is best to prepare for the swamp.

You have entered the quagmire that a Last Wife often traverses in her celestial journey. The muddle can be quite offensive at times. However, keep in mind that mud is not all bad. It can also be a healing agent and a choice skin care product. Although you may feel soiled by the dirt that can cling to you during your courtship, just think how pure your skin will be upon peeling off the mud mask.

You might be dreaming of slinging your own retaliation pie. My advice is not to get stuck in the muck but to bask in the glow the mud afforded you! After all, Cinderella's frock can be hand washed and look almost as good as new! And the rain boots—they are there to protect your crystal footwear.

BLINDED
BY LOVE

O kay, Lover Girl. Your New Man has you star-
tled, staggered, and swept off your feet!
The store clerk caught you scooping up
beauty tips and slipping *Cosmo* magazines under the
milk and potatoes in your grocery cart. You are busy
checking in at yoga studios to tighten your arm muscles and buttocks and announcing, "He may be The
One" to anyone who will listen.

Lingering over martinis with one of your girlfriends, you can hardly breathe as she asks, "You have
a New Man?"

Before you begin giddily describing your new
Sweetheart, you secretly wonder what her reaction
will be. *Will she be delighted for me? Or search my
purse during a bathroom break, steal his Facebook
address and "friend" him, offering to meet him for coffee when it's convenient?*

But the news is so good you don't care. This cannot wait. Besides, you have no reason to suspect

treachery. None of your past losers have even merited a yawn from her, and you are so tired of her pity. Wait 'til she hears *this*!

"Well, tell me," she coos, expecting another of your boring tales about the latest dud. You smugly smile and confess that there is so much to say you don't know where to start! But both of you know you'll try. Sex is first. You practically choke on your giggle. "He is so sexy—Angelina would leave Brad."

You can discern her fake smile—she is eaten up with jealousy!

Meanwhile, she is frantically wondering if she can find your college roommate's number on her cell phone, who is today one of her trusted therapists. You can hear it now, "Hilda? I'm here with our Mouse and she's delusional. I think she needs your evaluation."

Satisfied with the impact of your sexual analogy, you go on. "And He is sooooo funny. I turn off Jimmy Kimmel just to listen to his diatribes."

Your friend shares a weak giggle, not giving up on scheduling your upcoming $200 per hour visit with Dr. Help. Like the song says, she thinks you've been lonely too long!

"And smart," you continue. "This guy could upstage Bill Gates. He could have founded Microsoft, but it was not his cup of tea. Instead, He perfected his pecs and challenged Andrew Agassi at the Four Seasons bar.

At this, you say with a lovesick sigh, "I can't wait to see him in his tennis whites!"

You can hear it now, "Hilda? I'm here with our Mouse and she's delusional."

Your girlfriend's suspicion is growing and she's thinking, *I doubt I'll want anything to do with the loser.* That does it. With a disgusted huff, she slips off to the bathroom, ready to speed dial emergency services and report a lovesick sex kitten on the loose.

Your girlfriend's suspicion is growing and she's thinking, *I doubt I'll want anything to do with the loser.*

You clench your handbag and get ready to leave upon her return. You can discern her fake smile—she is eaten up with jealousy! *She will be the last one to meet my Man,* you tell yourself on the way home. He must be firmly in your loving arms before she attempts to pull him into her overly enhanced bazookas. No one will come between you and Sir Galahad!

IF HE'S RICH, YOU'RE A WITCH

Statistics never lie. Money is likely one of the reasons you are now positioned to assume the Last Wife's place. Doesn't the Bible tell us, "The love of money is the root of all evil"? You are about to find out! During your necking sessions with your new Rock, your Savior, and the Man of your Dreams (who was the man of *Her* dreams, and maybe a few before Her) He vows to you, and you to Him, "Money will *never* be an issue for us!"

When you exchange these words, be aware of your body at that point. The tightness in your jaw is not because of the TMJ you developed during your last life as a Last Wife (or potential Last Wife). That locked jaw is your brain telling you that you only wish it were so! This could be where you fall for your first big lie. Rest assured, Dreamboat is not oblivious to the almighty dollar! Whether you assumed your Last Wife position by death or divorce, you can be certain that money will be an issue.

Unless you discovered your Saint locked in a Tibetan monastery, you can bet He has money issues. If there's a lot of money to fret over, rest assured his concerns are not his alone. Whether He has secretly stashed stacks of greenbacks in a posh Switzerland account, or the non-descript vehicle circling his street turns out to be the private investigator employed by the last, Last Wife trying to nail him for past-due child support for his Precious Ones, He has money issues!

Whether or not you accept it, money has a lot to do with how you are treated as the Last Wife.

If you and your Honey are at a five-star dinner with the CEO of a New York City bank, you can bet these two discussed his millions earlier in the day. The greedy banker made his point, "How can we make sure it rots in my vault never to be touched by her manicured fingers? After all, money is meant to be inherited by your Precious Ones."

Your Scrooge realized, "He's right! This must not include any Tiny Tim not conceived through my loins. I've been successful in my own right as a man, and *my* Precious Ones stand to inherit!"

"After all, money is meant to be inherited by your Precious Ones."

Whether or not you accept it, money has a lot to do with how you are treated as the Last Wife. If Moneybags has already implemented an ironclad pre-nup that will control your every move, then whether He has pecs the size of Arnold, or the buzzards make a daily pass by the house just to see when his stretcher is rolled out for a potential feeding, money will be your soulmate.

So face it. If He's rich, you are a witch. I think that pretty much sums it up.

TIES THAT BIND

If you are one of the fortunate ones whose heretofore committed Stud Muffin has been lavishing you with over-the-top booty bounty, this could be bad. Step on the bathroom scale and record your fighting weight. You may need to bulk up for the arm wrestling and body blows that are looming in your future. The La Perla lingerie that He so deliriously delivered on Friday as you deftly slipped into your dancing shoes may be inadequate for the next phase of relationship bliss.

Once in the throes of his unparalleled charm and cunning remarks about your sexy smile, you may accidentally overlook it when He whispers, "We are going to need a prenup." Later, of course, you will replay every moment of the evening in your head, including his offhand remark. Did you hear him say we *need* a prenup? Your mind may jump to The Donald. Trump is probably the only one who will *need* another prenup. Surely, not my Man-Angel?

Your mind is buzzing, and the room is spinning. Suddenly, you realize the Rat has slipped something into the multiple martinis He insisted you swallow. You try to regain your composure even as your red La Perlas start pinching your cellulite. Of course, in the initial days of your courtship He assured you, "I don't see any cellulite, Honey." You suspect that He has since checked you out in the glaring sunlight and quietly shaved off one third of any assets He would share with you in the future. He knows that in order to have blissful consummation night after night, He will need to spring for your liposuction. And He happens to know a good plastic surgeon. This man is no fool!

What do you do now? You pray. You wait. You try to find your lawyer.

A tear comes to your eye as you think, *I am in over my head!* This is a good time to think about the one person you admire the most, your yoga instructor. She has prepared you for this moment. In times of extreme stress, you have learned to take deep, cleansing breaths . . . now, do it! With each labored breath, your devious Dinner Mate will simply think you are hot for him! This is good; let him think it.

The Sly Devil breathes deeply also, but his is a sigh of relief as He tells himself, *If she puts up a fight at some later date, my lawyers will do all the dirty work. I will just remind her that she affirmed her cooperation.* "But, Honey, don't you remember, we agreed the night I gave you the red lacy bra?"

What do you do now? You pray. You wait. You try to find your lawyer. *Where is he? At Gold's Gym again?* Don't begrudge him—this could work in your favor because he will need big muscles to protect you.

Still sitting at dinner, you suddenly hear an ominous craaack—is it a crack in your relationship, or is it just the term his lawyers will use to gain position and bargaining power when they tell your Prince Charming (or Don Juan) that you might be "cracking up"?

They'll say, "As your lawyers, we must tell you we believe you should shave another third from your assets because she is going to need therapy!"

And they may be right!

RINGS AND BLING

Is your engagement ring bigger than Hers? Everyone is going to ask. If that is the case, do you strut around with your big diamond shining in Her kids' faces? You know the question the Ex is dying to ask—"What kind of ring did Daddy get her?"

If your friends mistake your engagement ring for a crystal paperweight, and your body weight increases by a percentage point once it's on your finger, it might be said of you, "She's a gold digger."

Everyone will think you hit pay dirt before the big day. You can bet that after you ran into Her old girlfriends at the deli they whipped out an iPhone and asked Siri to dial up his Ex.

"You won't believe it!" they'll chirp. "Her ring is the size of a strawberry! Keep your eyes open—your alimony check is in jeopardy. No way can this joker pay you *and* pay for that ring. Call your lawyer!"

If, on the other hand, He suggests a crafty strategy like, "Honey, let's buy matching bands," the cheap rascal is probably trying to buy you off. What can you say to that without looking as if you really are a scheming gold digger?

"Okay . . . " you gulp weakly. This is especially painful if you have already discovered that your True Love mortgaged the farm to buy his Last Wife the Elizabeth Taylor Hope Diamond! Does He just not love you enough? You choke back the tears.

Upgrading that puppy will be your first order of business.

Your Sly Lover may even decide that you have no right to determine the 4 Cs of his purchase. The cut is irrelevant in his mind, and clarity, color, and carat weight are not vital to his financing plan. One night, He ceremoniously slips it on your finger during his emotional declaration, "I will love you forever!" You suspect there might be a stone somewhere on the top of your fourth finger, so you feign being overcome by your love for him and slink off to the bathroom where the light is better.

~~~~~~~~~~

Does He just not love you enough? You choke back the tears.

~~~~~~~~~~

If He thinks this little nothing will do, just wait 'til after the wedding, you say to yourself. Upgrading that puppy will be your first order of business. Your Saturdays will be spent designing your one-year anniversary ring—that is, if He ever wants to have sex again!

COUGARS
AND KITTENS

So, you have taken the road less traveled and fallen for a young and studly Ladykiller, still wet behind the ears and other unmentionable places. My, my, my. How shall you handle this, you wanton Jezebel?

Every time you jump giggling into bed, knowing this romp has the potential for a half marathon, does the Pope later invade your pleasant dreams with a decidedly disappointed frown? Can you detect his stern admonishment amidst the pleasant sensations still lingering in your head from the last lively session with your tender Beefcake?

Does the pontiff think you're much too old for this emerging tot? It's true—you could be his mother, or at least a much older sibling. You better stop this lustful behavior and repent before your sins of the flesh are too visible to your brethren!

The Pope is right! you admit, tossing and turning until the morning hours. The only place you can win is when you are cavorting with your budding Adonis. Everywhere you turn, you are screwed (albeit in a different place)!

Your girlfriends' frequent trips to the powder room during the breathless descriptions of your bedroom frolics are not due to weakened bladders. They simply need a chance to reapply makeup over the tear tracks. When you confess, "He's so fit, I don't think He *ever* gets tired!" they may smile, but their envy cannot be concealed as they reflect on their Mr. Right waiting for them at home.

The only place you can win is when you are cavorting with your budding Adonis.

They may even wonder if your Budding Beast is just simpleminded. *Surely He can see her need for Botox*, one thinks. Another silently cries, *She needs it a lot more than I do. What gives?*

The general, unspoken consensus at your regular 9:00 a.m. Starbucks get-togethers is that you may be his Mrs. Robinson at night, but you'll be his Maggie May in the harshness of morning. A few Sunday mornings sans dull hangovers and they're figuring He'll dump you.

What is He like? Is He romantic? They are dying to know it all.

She'll get what she asked for! they conclude as you naively head to the counter to pick up your skinny latte. *Who does she think she is?* And yet, you can take heart because even Jimmy Fallon's monologue won't be able to distract from their unseemly task of faking yet another orgasm later that night.

We all dream of the supportive, got-your-back back girlfriends who text and email you constant encouragement and positive vibes. They are the ones who show unwavering interest and curiosity regarding your Lover. *What is He like? Is He romantic?* They are dying to know it all. If your new conquest doesn't work out, these YaYa Sisters will be the ones to conduct a séance, mortally wounding him and propelling you into Cupid's arms for your next tryst. Woman Power has you firmly in its bosom.

Wrong! Wake up, sister.

You can bet most women worth their salt who are not already pushing the sheets with another hunk would trade places with you and provide the silk pillowcase to boot. The competitive factor between women, especially single women, rivals any blood sport. With Samurai Swords drawn, they stand ready to take you out at a moment's notice. If you really do have a soul sister who can sing "We Are Family," count yourself extremely lucky.

Hold tightly to his flaccid mid-section—you are in for some rough remarks.

Your guy friends, however, are impressed. *Wow, she must really be a good lay!* they think to themselves. *I wonder how old she really is? Who cares? She looks pretty good for her age, whatever it is!* Yes, Madame Cougar, men are so dense!

With Samurai Swords drawn, they stand ready to take you out at a moment's notice.

On the other hand, if the nightclub bouncer stops you Lovebirds at the door and insists on proving you are legal and your handsome escort pulls out his senior discount card, you could be labeled the kitten with the alley cat! Although true love has no boundaries, and we've all heard, "age doesn't matter," expect some raised eyebrows! Hold tightly to his flaccid mid-section—you are in for some rough remarks.

Can you believe how young she is?
We all know what she's after . . .
and it's not his body!
We all know what He's after . . . her body!
How disgusting, trying to relive his youth.
She must be desperate to be with him!
I bet He pops Viagra!

Your aging Lord of the Manor thinks nothing of introducing the family to his trophy. After all, they will surely see immediately how much the two of you are in love. He can hear the accolades now for having picked a delectable queen for his castle. No unsightly bulges under the caftan for this frisky, young feline.

If you really do have a soul sister who can sing "We Are Family," count yourself extremely lucky.

Your family is not so sure. They assume He's gonna die a long time before you're ready for the plowed field. You'll have to raise the kids by yourself.

"Will you get his social security?" they want to know. "If so, how much is it?"

Face it, Barbie, your Ken is graying and fraying. He's into Sinatra and you want Justin Timberlake. You order a dirty martini and He orders a shot of Mylanta. You are having a mid-afternoon snack while He is downing his last soft diet before early-to-bed. Close your eyes at bedtime as He crawls between the sheets and asks for another blanket. You still have a ways to go before your hot flashes.

On the upside, your body's imperfections will no longer be important as you accompany him to the cataract surgeon.

If your unlined skin and tight thighs are made of alligator, and you don't mind the arrows flung your way from everyone (and I do mean everyone), you could be in safe terrain. As you are thrust headlong into a previous generation, stock up on reading material, especially the latest issue of *AARP* magazine. Make sure his cardiologist is now a "favorite" in your contact list. On the upside, your body's imperfections will no longer be important as you accompany him to the cataract surgeon. Just ask yourself before you plunge into the land of the elderly, "Do I really enjoy Sunday afternoons spent with his friends at Golden Acres?"

IT'S RAINING SOIREES

If you have had at least one wedding shower, make it the last. It is considered gauche to have multiple showers for multiple weddings. You surely have the requisite mixer, blender, and carving knife.

I know, it is really tempting to whisk over to the nearest Williams-Sonoma and add your name to the bridal lists so all of your well-wishers will bestow more goodies on the happy couple. And I know what you're thinking: "Darn, an opportunity missed."

Miss this one. Any announcement blaring, "We will soon be merging households" should be sans any reference to "The couple is registered at . . . "

If you pale at the thought of no new treasures and having to mix your smoothies with his avocado green blender, simply make the best of it, Pollyanna. Or open a new joint account at Target and feather your own nest.

In regard to lingerie showers, Girls—don't fool yourselves. The rules are simple for a happy Prince:

If you're under 30, you need to wear nothing at night!

If you're 30–45, his white shirt and flannel pants will suffice as your flesh might be a little softer than you'd like.

50 and over: Wear the 30–45 year old attire, just dim the lights.

Over 65: I suggest total darkness and no gifts. Even gag gifts make us gag at a certain age. No need to rub salt in the wounds!

"We will soon be merging households" should be sans any reference to "The couple is registered at . . . "

A CIVIL
UNION

The wedding, what a minefield! This is often where the real drama starts. William Shakespeare did not give us much of a revelation when he wrote, "The course of true love never did run smooth." The path to planning the perfect day has never been easy, and believe you me, the petal-strewn walk down the aisle will be no bed of roses either!

"Honey, you can have any kind of wedding you want . . . " he may whisper to you in the early stages of bliss. Don't fall for this as you fall into his arms. Be as wary as an alley cat eyeing a bowl of milk placed by a fence. You want a big wedding at a romantic destination or in a sweet, simple chapel, while He wants his ex brother-in-law (his best friend!) to be his best man. This is part of the big bag of trash you both bring to the relationship that sometimes can never be disposed of, but perhaps can at least be compacted.

Regardless of the location, your special day is likely to be an assembly of friends, foes, and dysfunctional family: His, yours, Hers, and theirs! This celebration brings out the best and the beastly! Your perfect day will be analyzed and scrutinized from all sides.

His female friends, especially the ones He bedded or potentially bedded, will be furious. There is no better description—they are all up in arms and wondering what kinds of tricks you pulled to get him.

If you are marrying money, her newly flossed porcelains are ready.

She probably gripped him with her great oral hygiene . . . what a slut! one thinks to herself as she holds the wedding invitation in hand. Still another affirms her wedding day strategy to her closest confidante, "I'll go to the wedding, look simply fab, be mean to Her, and He will wish it were me He is whisking off my Manolo Blahniks!"

And you can just hear his family's reactions now.

"Our little angel is marrying *Her*," bemoans his vigilant mother, protecting her cub. "No surprise to me," says Great Gramma Lil. "I just hope She's not in the family way!"

Mama Bear, in shock that her poor son is taking on the Kate Gosselin brood, whispers back, "I don't know how he'll ever make this bunch a living. I tell you one thing, she better not expect me to babysit one minute. It's not *me* getting into this mess—it's my husband's son."

They are all up in arms and wondering what kinds of tricks you pulled to get him.

Your mother is likely to be in one of two states at this point. If you are marrying money, her newly flossed porcelains are ready. "I just love my new son-in-law," she will beam to everyone within earshot. Is it the smell of her brand new perfume purchased for the Big Day, or her syrupy bragging to her friends (whose children married assorted losers) that is creating a wave of nausea rampant in the room?

Dressed to the nines but with somber expressions, they know this could be the end.

On the other hand, your mother's bouts with depression could reappear. If your Soon-to-be-Betrothed invited your father to accompany him to Men's Warehouse to pick up his one-day tuxedo rental (and his mother offered to bake homemade meat loaf to serve at the rehearsal dinner), your mother will be forced to consider renewing her Valium prescription.

To his crowd, a place setting means deciding which place at the table they can grab the fastest to wolf down another Frito pie! *Here comes another freeloader,* your mother thinks, wishing she could get a refund on your private school tuition. *When she ends up throwing neighborhood parties in her doublewide, all the scrimping I did to pay for her sorority gown will prove needless,* she laments.

At the wedding rehearsal, the mothers-in-law try never to come close enough to rub any body parts together, including hugs or handshakes. Even though flu season has long passed, these two act like quarantined athletes ready for a fight. The slightest spark of competition can send the two mama bears into a sparring match while their two cubs receive last-minute instruction from the clergy.

. . . your mother will be forced to consider renewing her Valium prescription.

His children are freshly spit-shined from the saliva his Ex-wife has spewed. Their processional resembles Mary Queen of Scots going to the executioner. Dressed to the nines but with somber expressions, they know this could be the end. She has assured them, "Daddy is hooking up with the ugly stepmother. My darlings, you're toast! You will be lucky to get a Walmart special next Christmas—it will be the one thing left that her kids didn't want."

Just then, the bitter enemy approaches—the Last Wife's Best Friend!

You've threatened your children, "Do not make a scene." They are at their Sunday best. Little smiling cherubs or teenage starlets, they will put on an Oscar-worthy performance. "Mommy, we are so glad to be at the ball. You look so pretty," they chime together. (At this, the thought briefly occurs to you that maybe you shouldn't have divorced their father since your genes so evidently worked to perfection!)

At the reception, both families jockey for the best position in the buffet line. The shoving and hissing among the bloodlines might be clandestine, but be certain it's there.

Another wedding . . . at least the food looks good, the family misfits think as they gnaw on another beef rib. "Oh well," mutters cousin Bernie. "Even if my top button snaps, I am eating another round. Moneybags can pay for it."

Here comes another freeloader, your mother thinks, wishing she could get a refund on your private school tuition.

Just then, the bitter enemy approaches—the Last Wife's Best Friend! She has been angling all night for a direct hit, one that can land you where you belong. She and the Last Wife have practiced their moves during their "just-one-more-glass" pity parties throughout your engagement. If she could not get to you before the priest marries you off, she will get to you during the conga line!

By now, your face is beginning to freeze into an eternal "say cheese" position. "What are you smiling for?" she spits. Shocked into reality, you realize permanent lines have now formed around your grin even as you think, *How I hate this witch.*

Suddenly your charm school training kicks in. "We know you are so happy for us," you say as you squeeze your Beloved's arm.

Thank God the ring is tightly wound around your finger!

Hyperventilating and unable to reply, she skulks off and later expresses her disappointment with a text to his Last Wife: "She is still standing. But I won't give up. I am just like family and you can count on me."

Thank God the ring is tightly wound around your finger! This battle is over, but the war has just begun.

THE NEST:
YOURS, MINE
OR HERS?

Has your Lovebird already constructed a nest or two for his former Turtledoves before you arrived? There is a high probability He loves living in the big oak tree just the way it is. His Ex may do a flyby occasionally to check out if you've changed things—and surely for the worse.

Although you may wince when the twigs left over from his former Beloved prick your love-primed buttocks, your Intended has said on more than one occasion, "My place is just the way I like it." Uh-oh. Is that faint smell wafting through his bedroom Her Chanel No. 5, or a rotten core from the last Chickadee who was the apple of his eye?

Okay, Princess. Don't even think of entering his lair until He at least changes the sheets. Even if He brags, "I just bought expensive new linens," don't be fooled. Realize that these are not for you, oh Cherished One. They are to cover up any sign of the last Canary who left flying south.

Instead, what if your nest is the perfect abode? You have spent years fine-tuning your bungalow to your liking. Yours is the one place that has provided comfort after fruitless forages into the singles-bar jungles or countless church socials. As you staggered in your front door night after futile night, you always found refuge there as you hysterically searched eHarmony into the wee morning hours. Could He possibly be planning to alter *your* roost?

Where do the newest snapshots of you two squeeze in?

Whether He invades your idyllic homestead, or you choose to settle into his nest (despite constant jabs from leftover reminders of the former female resident), this is a big decision! If you settle in his man cave, expect complications.

"Not to worry, my precious Lover," He may whisper. "You can change the house however you want. I want it to be *yours!*"

These are the famous last words to a Last Wife's ears. Take some advice from those who have been there. Tread as lightly as an army sergeant traversing the weeds in Cambodia. There is a buried explosive device ready to detonate if you so much as move his jock strap!

If you settle in his man cave, expect complications.

Which family portraits get the bigger spotlight, the best places in the house? Do images of the Ex stay? Will their bygone Disney vacation pics enjoy a permanent place in the hall? Where do the newest snapshots of you two squeeze in?

Don't attempt to replace any pictures without his expressed approval, even if they are of his 1968 prom sweetheart's bouffant or his frat brother smoking a reefer in holey underwear. Pictures are sacred—but only the ones taken before you, Last Wife. If morning after morning you sit down to a peaceful breakfast and stare at the same photo frame housing his former goateed brother-in-law and his Last Wife's nephew, say a daily prayer: "I will learn to love these strangers. I will, I will . . . "

If Lover Boy insists on living at your place, the rules are simple. Question his loyalty first, his asset base second. Don't be fooled when He readily gives up the apartment He shared with the last Honey so He can easily settle in with you. Yours is a man of questionable loyalty.

~~~~~~~~~~~~~~~~~~~~

This sucker is not bagged yet. In fact, you must be aware that you might be the next Last Girlfriend.

~~~~~~~~~~~~~~~~~~~~

You may wonder if your highly mobile Inamorato will surge from your coop with a curious look in his eye whenever a new wave of comely chickens flies over. Does the least flutter ruffle his feathers? Your Man may be suffocating in the trees you call home. Some men need to soar like an eagle (if only to swoop down on the next unsuspecting victim).

Watch for the telltale signs of commitment during the coupling stage. When you suggest you should leave some things at his house, and He temporarily stops breathing, you can bet there is another Chickadee sleeping in the nest or circling the tree above. If He's going to see "old friends" in Palm Springs, or heading to another Big Twelve weekend, keep your roving eyes roving. You have competition! This sucker is not bagged yet. In fact, you must be aware that you might be the next Last Girlfriend.

Question his loyalty first, his asset base second.

Just when you think your relationship is getting hotter and He pours you another glass of wine, He may slyly add, "I think we both need some space." This means your Wily Coyote is searching for new prey, or worse yet, He already has another female deer in his sights. If you are smart and not too blind to his insidious plan, you will agree that He *does* need his space. And, Honey, you will need yours, too. Make room in your nest for the next one. You can bet the sky is full of them—you just need to grab your binoculars and get in the path of the next Eagle's eye!

Whatever you decide to do, please don't change the name on the gas bill. It could get mighty cold in your domicile, and I predict the current Cad won't be there long!

THE EVIL
EMPIRE

*(Or The Women That
Didn't Get Him Club)*

I n *Star Wars,* Princess Leah, dressed in flowing white caftans, won the heart of Luke Skywalker. Her journey to love wasn't easy, laden with battles and narrow escapes on many occasions. Somehow, the Princess kept her air of grace and strength (and cinnamon bun curls) intact, knowing Darth Vader and the Evil Empire lurked just beyond her Kingdom.

But that was the movies. When it comes to modern romance, the Evil Empire is formed by a crafty potpourri of characters—members of The Women That Didn't Get Him Club! This seething coterie began to gel as each one turned to her favorite casserole recipe in her loose-leaf binder. Each one dreamed of walking in your ruby red slippers one day. As they boldly asked their friends to set them up, they felt certain they could take it from there.

Waiting patiently as He finalized his last divorce, each one pondered the exact best timing to pounce like a frenzied tigress. They fret that He may soon be out there frolicking with some nameless harlot while they are home stoking the fire just to keep their flame from extinction. Day after day, they pull off another calendar page . . . has it been long enough?

Soon, they sense a shadowy figure is swirling around their intended kill. It's you, the soon-to-be Last Wife! "Darn! She's already got a lock on him," they hiss. "Foiled again!"

At their informal encounters during various social gatherings, they circle like vultures looking for weakened prey.

Although their unseemly intentions are hidden from the rest of the world, they form a devious union, The Women Who Didn't Get Him Club. The members endure their disappointment in silence until one utterance spews forth at your wedding reception, "She sure moved in fast!" They all nod in agreement and ceremoniously rip a cuticle hoping to extract a small drop of blood and seal the deal as blood sisters. Their one goal? To uncover and flaunt the weaknesses of the One Who Got Him to the world. The cause is bigger than just your circle of influence; the entire universe must know.

At their informal encounters during various social gatherings, they circle like vultures looking for weakened prey. They smile as they wish you well. "How's it going?" they ask. All the while, they are wishing for a tsunami to swallow you up. If by chance you are taken out, they may yet have another turn at the trough.

Their one goal? To uncover and flaunt the weaknesses of the One Who Got Him to the world.

"Can it really be so? I lost out again?" they cry, trying not to think about how they missed another one. The furrows in their foreheads deepen as they spend their nights worrying over their fate.

"Let me be next!" they pray. "I must not, I *will not* let another get away."

WHOSE KIDS ARE THESE, ANYWAY?

Whose kids are these, anyway? Your steps, his steps, adopted steps? Doesn't matter. Just beware: repeated stomping on your toes produces giant blisters. Whoever coined the term, "stepchildren" must have been bleeding profusely from the wounds inflicted by the little Darlings. The first thing to determine as you are eyeballing your Prince, dreaming of the Princess crown, is what strategy his kids are scheming in regards to you. Detour? Delay? Denial? Or the most noble game of all . . . Derail?

Now, if you have been warned about their bloodline, don't be a blind fool. Is there a plan to knock you off because you're bold enough to risk getting near the golden cushion? Are they the nieces and nephews of Godzilla, or are they truly the cherubs of a goddess? You need to be careful, even if they sing your praises to the heavens and fly on gilded wings. Jeweled scabbards can hold switchblades, and diamond-crusted bullets still sting.

No Last Wife, regardless of her celebrated attributes, can come close to their Sainted Mother. Don't even try. Think of yourself as the Mother of the Groom at every family event. Regardless of the nature of the feast, you are expected to sit a lot, smile a lot, and shake your head up and down a lot.

Recalling your past losers, they want to know what *this* joker's like.

Remember, beige *is* the color wheel as far as your wardrobe is concerned. If you have any Victoria's Secret stash left over from the romantic phase between you and their father, better that it stays in a locked closet with the lavender-scented shelf liner. Wear armor around the house. I suggest baggy clothes, showing no hint of cleavage unless yours happen to flop. Shaking and flopping are both good and desirable stepmother assets. Above all, never let a clever or engaging moment surface. Those slips can be mighty damaging. And brains? No brains. Brains are not a good thing.

Ah, you think, *but ours could be a later-in-life fairy tale.* "There will be no problems," you've already assured each other. "Our children are grown." However, grown children (though possessing scattered gray hairs and facial wrinkles) do not ensure familial bliss. In fact, the mind games played at this level can be more honed and devious.

Above all, never let a clever or engaging moment surface.

Your own children may worry their mom is making a big mistake, but they think, "We can't tell her a single thing." Recalling your past losers, they want to know what *this* joker's like. Your Angel daughter may roll her eyes as she tells her friends, "I have to meet Mom's new boyfriend on Sunday." She still doesn't understand "why Mom had to leave Dad" and she feels sorry for him. "Well, I will be nice," she vows, "but nobody is as good as Daddy. Sometimes I hate my mother!"

If your sons are meeting their PNF (Potential New Father), they are more likely to be a little easier on him. Can He shoot a few baskets, and does He watch football? That's all they need to know. It's a real plus if He has a great media room where they can crash and watch ESPN. Besides, if their dad is the kind that is always out chasing women their age, having a father around the house (doesn't matter whose house) might not be so bad.

The ultimate insult cuts deep: "And never will she get one of the family recipes!"

Prepare to be inspected like a mixed breed at the Westminster Dog Show by all of his kids. They may opine something like, "I don't see what He sees in Her. Mom is so much classier." Or it may come straight out as, "She just wants his money" (understand this is the case even if He is a flat broke womanizer with a bad toupee).

It's a real plus if He has a great media room where they can crash and watch ESPN.

"I will have to say hello when she's around," one may confess. "But never, ever am I going to go out of my way to talk to her." "I will just stay in another room at family gatherings," vows another. The ultimate insult cuts deep: "And never will she get one of the family recipes!"

His grown sons may whistle something to the tune of, "Hey, did you see Dad's new girlfriend? Scary!" Or if you're reasonably pretty, "Hey, did you see Dad's new girlfriend? Wow, what does she *see* in *him*?"

Welcome to the family!

THE PERFECT
PROGENY

While ascending to the position of the Last Wife, you just know there are sooooo many happy times ahead! One of the pleasantries you most look forward to is introducing your own genetic perfection into the mix.

"My children . . . " Doesn't the sound of saying it bring warm thoughts to mind? *My little ones. The girls. My boys. The family.* You know you've already produced the perfect family. (Their father, your ex-husband, that's a different story . . . but, like Scarlett, you will think about that another day.)

There is no doubt in your mind that everyone on his side (don't be fooled, this is a wrestling match with everyone jockeying for the best position) will instantly adore your little Shirley Temple. When they welcome your fair-haired Opie into their arms, you will feel as if you are finally in Mayberry. Aunt Bea will come through the door any minute with a fresh-baked cobbler and ask, "Who's hungry?" Or was that a scream from your Betrothed's mother, "She has *kids*?"

On the appointed day, you attempt to introduce his family (which you affectionately know as the Little Hellions) to your Angels. His brood looks treacherous. How dare they stare at your Goldilocks as if she is Honey Boo Boo? And your Little Prince is treated like Edward Scissorhands! Deep down in your gut, you feel a twinge that is not due to acid reflux. You suspect a battle is brewing. Still, you think that if you masquerade your voice into a Mary Poppins singsong, surely everyone will eventually be genuinely delighted with the new set-up.

Meanwhile, you are wondering exactly where your Pillar went.

It's beginning to dawn on you how that nasty last, Last Wife has set you up. "Just because Daddy is remarrying, you do not have to like those Little Aliens," she must have preached to her children. "No matter how nice they are to you, it is fake. Do you want to have no Daddy?"

The brainwashing continues, "Daddy's New Wife is just trying to replace you, and Daddy is letting it happen. Maybe with my help, you and Mommy can make them go away." "You are so strong," she tells them, "just like your Mommy. Now go out there and fight! Don't look at them. And surely don't talk to them."

How dare they stare at your Goldilocks as if she is Honey Boo Boo?

Meanwhile, you are wondering exactly where your Pillar went. Your Rock turns into putty even as his kids declare WWIII. He can only defend his children in a whiny voice, "They take a while to warm up. Honey, they will be okay." What about your Darlings? What did they do to have to defend their country? They aren't even old enough for the draft.

Your private Heaven has now become more like Dante's Inferno. You tell yourself things will be better if only you can get your Beloved away from the misfits. "They must be just like their mother . . . hateful and spiteful. Clearly, they could not have anything but the tiniest of sperm from the Man I Love." Gurgle, gurgle. Once again, your acid reflux is bubbling up.

THE LONG ARM OF THE SISTERS-IN-LAW

By law, you may have a new sister, a new family. It could be his sister, Her sister-in-law or sisters-in-law of the precious stepsons and stepdaughters. Or it could be a sister-in-law of a sister-in-law. Should I go on? Regardless of the configuration, there are many types of in-laws and some have had several faces. There are three basic kinds:

Organic. She is merely a split chromosome and has the same soul of your Soulmate. Therefore, she must protect her genes at all cost. If possible, she works to be a she-he clone of him. She often brags at the spring tea, "My brother and I are sooooo close." Translation: there is no air left for you to breathe, Cinderella!

Expect a dagger hidden somewhere in her Louis Vuitton. She has used it before and will use it again if anyone tries to suck blood from her Precious One. The ire and pain she can inflict is often compared to that inflicted by General Patton: it hurts long and hard.

As the Germans learned at considerable expense, the General will roll over anyone. Eva Braun, the long-time companion of Hitler, and Cinderella are the same easy target—they can both be wiped out with a single blow.

She wears a saintly smile because she knows, but ceases to warn the new kid on the throne, that this is gonna get ugly!

The Competitive One. This relative is the most interesting. Often Chanel clad, impeccably attired, and scheming for her place in the family tree, she thrives on the memories of her home life as a child with your Adored. Unfortunately, she harbors hate and resentment because her brother treated her badly and picked on her just because the bully could.

What's more, she is still mad at her neglectful mother who always loved him more. No one understands her pain. You, the newest entry into her tortured world, can be of use. She sees you as an ally, one who can suffer alongside her. You must be warned about his past. Perhaps together you can mount a campaign to reveal his warts to the world, since God knows He has fooled everyone up to now. You need her like you need the dagger from the Organic's precious leather tote.

The situation is akin to the Art of War strategy. When you are ahead, dominate. When behind, retreat. Believe me, if you fall behind, your status will be at the back of the bus with the toilet. If that happens, go there, lock the door, and chant Buddhist musings about peace and love while you gather your thoughts!

You, the newest entry into her tortured world, can be of use.

The Invisible One. There are those rare times that the new sister-in-law becomes a quiet supporter. She remembers how it was for the first Last Wife and possibly the second Last Wife. She wears a saintly smile because she knows, but ceases to warn the new kid on the throne, that this is gonna get ugly!

"Let's all get along," says Mother Teresa as she sets out the Monopoly board on the center of the dining room table.

She is truly a Godsend! This is not an overstatement. If the Invisible One always has your back, don't blow it! Stay at her side when the Organic says, "You are sooooo lucky to have my brother. Every woman in town was after him!" Grab her hand for support when the Competitive One slithers over to you in her newest Armani and says, "I think I wear a smaller size than you. You need my latest diet."

Cinderella may be whacked time and again, but the Invisible One will simply smile at you as she imparts her wisdom, "Honey, I know you can take it."

"TRUST"
FUNDS

I f your Prince is a highly endowed trust fund baby, remember what Jackie Onassis professed when questioned on her marriage to a distasteful little Greek man. She informed inquiring minds that Ari resembled Paul Newman when perched on his stacks of greenbacks! If the banks refer to your Beloved as the heir or the spare, you can bet that a bespectacled, hunchbacked CPA and several bloated trust attorneys are working overtime to burst your dreams of a Maserati. "Don't worry," declare their secret emails, *"a five-year-old C Class Mercedes will be the best she can hope for!"*

If the nest is to be feathered with his stash, expect a list of approved expenditures. The trust fund does not trust you, and you may find it untrustworthy as well. Excessive purchases upset the equilibrium of the beast, forcing it to tap you on the shoulder. Whether through a tersely worded note or your credit card being declined at Trader Joe's, enough is enough. When pushed to the limit, the money always wins; and never forget, Holly Golightly, Tiffany's can't be yours when it is his!

If, however, you are the fortunate one and the millions are yours because your hardworking immigrant father scratched someone's eyes out for it, you will need to be clear to the money-grubbing Opportunist. It is only fair to warn him that she who has the money makes the rules. I feel pretty . . . oh, so pretty!

"Honey, I won't stand in your way if you want to work. I know how much your independence means to you!"

"You'll see, Darling," you assure him, "being the Kept One is fun." His days of suffering are over (except for the torturous dinners with Daddy). Your Darling will no longer have to sport around town in a Ford Escort. You will clean him up like Carson, the butler, in Downton Abbey.

Your Beloved's job is so easy. Just say wonderful things about you and your family, never share a family secret, wait on you hand and foot and always remember your money is the boss. As the Last Wife, you must always be fair!

Of course, your Intended might simply be among the other 99 percent in America. Even if He is a working man, don't think money is not a part of your Casanova's psyche. Although your Romeo did not ask Juliet for a "ties that bind" prenuptial contract, you can believe that He is still concerned about money. Or his lack thereof.

As the Last Wife, you must always be fair!

As He sees it, once you are installed in his abode, you could become Ms. Paycheck, even though his birth name is not even similar to Johnny's, nor does He enthrall you with his country ballads. Shrewdly, He says to you, "Honey, I won't stand in your way if you want to work. I know how much your independence means to you!"

What a man, He is always putting you first!

Take note when your welcome home kiss from him gets less passionate by the day.

The actor Mae West once said, "Love conquers all, except poverty and a toothache!" The Last Wife can sometimes be the last best chance for the devious Interloper. Look for telltale signs that your Prince is not planning to shower you with fancy bobbles or to become your ticket to a paid-up MasterCard. Has He helpfully suggested that He should be added as an approved user on your card? This is the mark of the crafty Looker who wears the Armani blazer borrowed from his hard-working high school buddy. He promises to return it when his finances improve, meaning when your bank changes your checking to a joint account.

In the frenzy of emotions, you may nod your head and declare, "I don't care about money—our love is deeper than that!" You love your job and are convinced He will soon find something that is up to his level.

Keep your poster of Gloria Steinem near your desk because that is where you will be chained as your Man-child is enjoying daily three-hour lunches at the local bar searching the want ads. Take note when your welcome-home kiss from him gets less passionate by the day. He is already dreading your nightly chats.

"Love conquers all, except poverty and a toothache!"

"How was your day?" you ask as you set down your briefcase. "Did you find anything?"

Quick! What is my excuse today? He panics. *The witch never gives up! I want my mommy!*

If your daddy made sure that you can have any man you want without worrying the trust fund manager, you have a decision to make. Like the business icon determining if his new Last Wife is worth the prenup costs, you will sooner or later be forced to consider your potential partner's value to you. If your heart is overcome by the warmth of his embrace, you will be more than happy to finance his well-being (including his new Armani blazer). The feminists were right: having the money does give you the power!

KNIVES AND NEEDLES

I f your birth certificate affirms more than three decades behind you, the issue of plastic surgery and other maintenance requirements is likely paramount in your life. You have an urgent need-to-know about how to handle it!

Perhaps regular touch-ups at Dr. Look Good have resulted in your eternally rested facial expressions. Or maybe the scars you are hiding resemble mementos from a fierce battle in a smoky Mexican cantina. Either scenario piques the interest of his eager-to-know relatives. During short interchanges at his Thanksgiving dinner, his cousin (still wearing flesh-colored bandages from her eye lift) squints at your ears. She deftly brings up Aunt Myrtle's hatchet job from several decades ago and asks, "Don't you think plastic surgery has gotten *so* much better?"

You are on to this clandestine scheme. *But,* you realize, *I am going to have a hard time feigning my natural look.*

While sidling up to the holiday buffet, his brother sneaks a peak at your perfected décolleté straining against your silk blouse and suddenly bolts for the bathroom looking for his nitroglycerin tablets. Terrified of having yet another angina attack, he pops his pills and silently worries, *This woman may kill me!*

. . . if He is a wonderful person and full of love, so what if He is a little maimed?

Should you fess up to your Beloved? "Darling, I've had a little work. No one knows, but I want to be totally honest with you. You probably wouldn't have noticed as it didn't change me that much . . . "

Note that you should squint hard while you are confessing so you can spot any telltale scars around his ears. Run your hands through his hair to inspect any remnants of a toupee, paying close attention to any little bumps signifying implant rows. Moving right along, scrutinize his teeth for any clacking or movement, ugly black blobs signaling neglected dental visits or badly matched implants. Inspect him like a jockey inspects his steed at the Kentucky Derby.

After all, you want a sturdy horse and a smooth ride to the Winner's Circle.

Terrified of having yet another angina attack, he pops his pills and silently worries, *This woman may kill me!*

Feel no shame, Inspector Clouseau. You can bet He is ogling every inch of your body, too. Odds are your brazen Womanizer is carefully comparing you to his last conquest. So, if you've gone from small apples to large cantaloupes, and your Honey is eyeballing those perfect Cs, it might be time for you to come clean. Even though you might feel a bit squeamish telling him of your time under the knife, if He is part of the Big Boobs Boys Club, the bigger the better. It won't faze him a bit that a man has been there before!

If you do happen to discover any peculiar scars, scalp conditions, or cavities with your Beloved, your head may want your heart to rethink this. "He is damaged goods!" your brain may signal you. "It will take a small fortune just to keep him in working order." Your mind may even go to a weird place where you picture the two of you frolicking in bed . . .

What if his toupee swerves, or his dentures puncture my Cs? Can you catch cavities? You've got decisions to make, but if He is a wonderful person and full of love, so what if He is a little maimed?

FRIENDS
NEVER END!

His friends, Her friends, their friends, my friends, our friends, his kids' friends, your kids' friends . . . in a blended family, friends never end! Of course, they have your best interest in mind. They form early and instant opinions of your new relationship, which simply validates the old adage that opinions are like armpits—everybody has one.

Let's start with Her Friends. Here they come—many times in cloak and dagger. It is not just the gal pals who can inflict pain; the men involved can be just as sinister. Just when you think you are looking like a 10, they proceed to tell you about Her lovely eyes, Her kind manner or how She was a lively conversationalist. You are stopped dead in your stilettos as you half-listen to their recollections! But you thought Prince Charming told you she was Godzilla's older sister, complete with hairy armpits and unshaven legs? Oh, and the cellulite—it was simply unbearable for him.

Or worse, She may actually have been perfect in every way: wise, gorgeous, and fun. It is amazing to you that your Don Juan could have bagged the Perfect Woman. Regardless of how She got away, the fact remains that She is gone. He feels the loss and you might want to do the same. This may even be your opportunity to let your rearview mirror fog and say, "Hi ho, Silver. I am outta here!"

You smile and explain how great your Knight in Shining Armor is when suddenly around the aisle of designer dresses comes the Frenemy!

What about Your Friends? OMG! Do they ever shut up? They pontificate on your New Man every time you are together, wanting answers to their questions. Is He good in bed? What present did He buy you? Does He ever talk about Her? Depending on their mood, they might even chide you, "You could do better . . . " Or, "You should bag the sucker, just like She did."

His Kids' Friends may be quick to engage you in conversation if they're young, but their innocent friendliness might come with a price. While eating a snack you just served, one of them happens to say, "Mrs. Last Wife, Tommy's mommy could make the best homemade brownies I ever tasted." You'd like to stuff the dried-out Oreos you bought last week down his lying little throat.

They pontificate on your New Man every time you are together, wanting answers to their questions.

"Get outta here kid, this is my house," you want to say. But is it Her or his house, or theirs? Wow! Am I confused!

Worse yet, his grown-up kids' friends are capable of inflicting flesh wounds. They are coming, so be prepared. Here's a potential scenario. You are innocently shopping in a small boutique near your house. (Or is it his house? Her house? Here we go again . . .). The store clerk is deftly trying to identify if you are the potential new Last Wife. In that case, she'll be syrupy sweet as she has missed the commissions from the former Last Wife. You smile and explain how great your Knight in Shining Armor is when suddenly around the aisle of designer dresses comes the Frenemy! Beware, she is the Best Friend of your newly inherited daughter, the one with whom you are attempting to bond without much luck.

"Oh, so-and-so's mother was a size 2. I thought you were Her size!"

Nevertheless, you express delight at seeing her (having hopefully recognized her importance in the pecking order). She throws eye daggers at you, force-fully showing a slit of a tooth intended to suffice as a smile. With a glance at the new dress in your hand, she then lowers the boom. "Oh, so-and-so's mother was a size 2. I thought you were Her size!"

The store clerk is deftly trying to identify if you are the potential new Last Wife.

You hurriedly leave the size-six rack and throw up in the store bathroom. The "perfect brownie" is now lodged in your throat—or is that your psyche?

A BAD
DAY FOR
CINDERELLA

"**B**ut didn't Cinderella actually get her Prince Charming in the end?" you ask. Yes, but her glass slippers were cutting into her big toe after her stepmother and stepsisters nearly finished her off, innocently calling it just a healthy bleed.

What they don't tell you when you're a little girl about your fairytale romance is that Cinderella leaves the ball, glass slipper in shards! As the Last Wife . . . second, third, fourth, temporary, or permanent . . . you think you know your number, but believe me your status can change overnight.

Although you got to go to the ball and even danced with his former brother-in-law, who is still his best friend and bar buddy, beware. Prince Charming can turn into Don Juan while shopping for your first Valentine bouquet.

One sure sign is if the pricey roses wrapped in swaddling cloth that He used to lay at Cinderella's feet when you were dating have now turned into carnations inside a made-in-China Kroger discount special. Your 18-carat gold bobble is tarnishing quickly if He doesn't bother to remove the faded markdown tag blaring, "Goodbye Cinderella."

Is He already beginning his thrift plan, saving his dollars for the Next Last Wife? While you are pondering your disappointment with your spindly funeral corsage, keep in mind it could be the precursor to your fall from his grace.

Prince Charming can turn into Don Juan while shopping for your first Valentine bouquet.

His master plan may involve saving his money for the next big purchase—another bobble, but not for you. Watch out if at Christmas He craftily suggests to you, "Please don't get me anything. In fact, I think we should not buy each other gifts. We already know how much we love each other, and, gosh, there is nothing we need. Don't you agree?"

In reply, just give him the same amount of tooth in the same fake grin you received from your precious stepchild's Best Friend as she reminded you of your back fat. This is a bad day in the life of Cinderella!

THE OTHER MAN

OMG! This is dangerous terrain! A brother-in-law can be your ally, especially if you have a good bum he can lightly pinch when his wife or your Beloved is not near. Be assured, he secretly believes he is the one you really dream of every night.

A dimly lit family dinner with him is always a trip down memory lane. He boasts of his high school athleticism and his cheerleader conquests, all the time wondering how he can scoot his chair close enough to rub your thigh. His wife is disgusted the entire time, rolling her eyes and ignoring his obvious hyperbole. She is too busy being consumed with private thoughts about how she ended up with this fool. To distract herself, she occasionally envisions the raunchy sexcapades you must be having with her brother.

Never forget, testosterone from the same bloodline can be competitive. Your new almost-brother might be peeved if you still look voluptuous while his ball and chain's boobs sag like two bags of wet concrete. It is critical that you stay on the other side of the room at family events. Just breeze by him with a slight nod as he assumes his usual place at the head of the buffet line.

He may even deserve some genuine compliments if he cleared the way for you like Paul Bunyan.

Some of these types will volunteer to commandeer the bar. Better to skip the libations or risk lewd comments about your new sex life. This man is a dreamer, mostly of you and his brother. Whether his rotund torso greets you as he is pulling up his belt (which has now sunk to knee length), or his breath reeks like your neighbor's St. Bernard whenever he licks your cheek in a side kiss, he knows he is the real hunk around here. Is that green around his jowls the same sign of envy he suffered when your Stud made the football team and he was only invited to play afterschool badminton?

On rare occasions, your new brother-in-law can become the strongest member of your Last Wife support group. He has the potential to fully understand the contents of your new family's dysfunction. If this is the case, lean on him only in the direst situations, as he is likely already exhausted by the unseemly brew. He may even deserve some genuine compliments if he cleared the way for you like Paul Bunyan. If that is the case, invite him to dinner often and go out of your way to have him around during Thanksgiving. Your heart rate will slow when he puts the wayward nephew in his rightful place.

DEAR MAMA BEAR

Dear Next Mother-in-Law,

We have both been here before. Let me start by saying I am so excited to be in the Last Wife's position and to be your last daughter-in-law. Now, I don't expect you to love me. I don't even expect you to like me. But I do expect that you will always pick out my best attributes when your bridge friends ask how it's going. Although you may grind your teeth to a point that warrants your dentist's suggestion of a night guard, and your weekly massages turn into more serious visits to the chiropractor, I expect you to keep your negative opinions to your therapist.

Being a New Wife, I already have the odds stacked against me. His Perfect Ones (your Grandperfect Ones) are causing me bouts of colitis. My Little Angels are now pining to move in with my Ex, claiming they prefer their father's new Last Wife's scowls over our blended family "bliss." I really don't expect your sympathy or empathy. The best I can hope for is to receive no grandmother's recipes, no regifted holiday gifts, and certainly no pictures of you and his Last Wife on the family vacation to Florida. I understand you were close to her. After all, your Perfect One did choose her.

I see you eyeing me as if picking out the Sunday roast at Whole Foods, only I suspect you believe I'm not nearly so wholesome. I know you are baffled why your son cannot see the truth—namely, that I will age more quickly than him (thanks to your side of the family's genes). There are so many ways I don't measure up that you've lost count (although I realize Alzheimer's is out of the question in your family). You've silently vowed to do your best to hold your tongue, even when you feel the urge to set me straight—if only to make me love you more in the long run.

But I am not above begging for your forgiveness. I had no grand scheme to hook him, and I even ignored his flirtatious glances as he cunningly hid his left ring finger the first time we met. I admit I should have been at a more innocent establishment, and the numerous martini glasses in front of him should have alerted me: This man is on the prowl. Yes, I fell for him after he shared with me his lonely misery and assured me that he is not a deceitful, devious sort but a man desperate for love. Dear Last Mother-in-law, he even told me, "You are just like my mother." Who could not love that?

Regardless of the circumstances that got us to this place, we are now forced to coexist. Let's make peace. I am not a fighter unless my face is smashed into the mat. If the wrestling match gets ugly, I must warn you that in my single years I achieved a black belt in self-defense. My last mother-in-law was a tad bit bigger than you and appeared to be meaner, but God knows the truth will surface when I pin you for another victory!

With much love,

Your Last Daughter (in-Law)

DEAR
GOLDILOCKS

Dear Goldilocks,

As you are my Baby Bear's about-to-be Last Wife, I am slightly concerned. No, absolutely horrified. I lie awake at night in a cold sweat (unrelated to my decades-long hot flashes), popping antacids and wondering what kind of debacle my Perfect Darling has ended up in this time.

I know he thinks you are the One (again) and is willing to jump out of a ship, swim the ocean and forego his relationship with his Perfect Mother (well, we know that last bit isn't true) just to keep you in the sack. After all, he is a little bit like his father, may he rest in peace, the oversexed oaf.

I am still exhausted from all the questions about his last divorce. Yes, I know that you think my bridge group ladies are merely sympathetic do-gooders, but let me tell you—things are not what they seem! New gossip makes them salivate. When I announced that my former daughter-in-law and son were splitting, they could hardly choke down the lemon bars quick enough to start the bantering, their neck waddles quivering with anticipation to hear the next episode in the soap opera. Even the people in my weekly group therapy sessions want to know who my son is "banging" and if his new girlfriend is "pure trash." (What kind of New Age talk is this? I don't feel well.)

As a mother who gave up everything for my Precious One, I ask myself what I did to deserve this. His escapades with all you women have cost me countless emotional breakdowns. Night after night, I dream I am a poodle in a room of pit bulls, all of your rabid mothers encircling me. "Your son better be good to my daughter," one howls. At this, the rest bare their jowls, poised and ready to tear at my flesh.

When I think of my son spending holidays with your Duck Dynasty *when he could be with his mother at* Downton Abbey *and my cultured clan, I can hardly bear it. But go ahead, I can't stop you from taking control.*

Although your calculated and covert maneuvers may have reeled in my foolish offspring, I refuse to be duped. When we engage in our obligatory encounters, just know that my aging eyes see you for what you are—a Queen Bee luring suitors into your hive. My son just happened to fly too close to your throne.

To be continued, I'm sure,

Your "Last" Mother-in-Law . . . Ha!

SHE OR ME— WHO'S IN THIS TREE?

Do we *have* to talk about the Exes? Why does someone always have to ask about the Last Wife? "Have you ever met Her? What is She like? How long have they been divorced?" If the Former Wife has passed, the questions are even more intrusive: "What did She look like? How long ago did She die? Did She have a tragic disease?" In the case of divorce, it's no holds barred: "So, how hideous *was* She anyway? The questions keep spilling over you like a hostess accidentally dropping a glass of wine at dinner. As a Last Wife, I am offering a suggestion to Last Wives everywhere: wear dark colors because you will get spilled on.

As the soon-to-be Last Wife, you are like Paris Hilton at New York Fashion Week—you know you are the Princess of the moment. Hold on tight. You are about to enter insecurity hell! One day, the Love of Your Life utters an innocuous compliment about his Last Fabulous One and having loved her coffee cake. This He happens to mention over the runny egg breakfast that you woke at 6:00 a.m. in order to serve him. And you are not a morning person. How dare He not be appreciative of your Herculean efforts!

What about all the dinners you endure in order to bond with their old friends? The $100 bottle of vino your Lover orders to take the edge off doesn't quell the banter between the odd couple sitting next to you and your team.

Your small donation to his psyche looks like Mt. Everest in comparison.

"Remember when we all went golfing in Pebble Beach?" the man mentions, recalling times gone by with the last, Last Wife and your Beloved. "She is a great golfer." Oblivious, his wife throws in, "You two looked so cute in the golf cart. Are you still playing?"

You scowl your displeasure. This is getting old fast.

When they suggest the two of you go out to play this Sunday, you smile and silently recall the last time you played golf and your supreme concern about the mating squirrels on the green. Your laughable tee off can turn even the most empathetic teammates into laughing hyenas. The Ex wins again—your handicap is close to your age and Hers is nearly negligible. Oh well, at least golf is not that important to your new Last Love.

What about all the dinners you endure in order to bond with their old friends?

The worst night of your life is the one when you ran into Her and Her new hunk and watched your Sweetest Thing turn into a tortured mass of nerves. He could hardly utter an introduction. "Hello," she purred like a satisfied kitten. And you? Your throat tightened so quickly that you could barely get a sip of water to trickle down.

"Hi," you finally squeaked, feeling every bit the insecure, worthless, and unaccomplished Woman now in his life.

Take heart, She is not coming back for at least two reasons. One, take a look at the Newbie's rippled pecs straining against his tee shirt. She has moved on, emphasized by how the Ferrari roared as they split the scene—their sexual chemistry leaving lasting impressions of yet another Sunday afternoon in a heated series of yoga poses. The other reason? Your

Man could no longer stand her perfection. His feelings of ultimate inadequacy are good for you. Your small donation to his psyche looks like Mt. Everest in comparison. He can quickly get used to your charity. Take heart, Mother Teresa, you are in a good place!

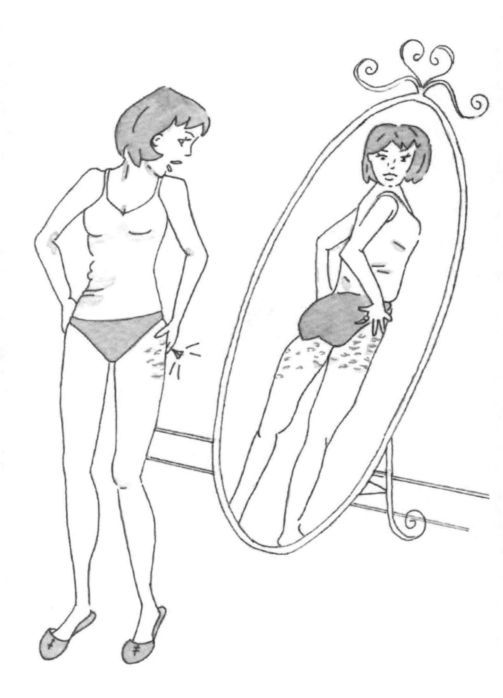

CINDERELLA
HAS
CELLULITE

How did I get here? What happened to the fairytale dreams, and why is my Prince Charming taking me to the WWF wrestling match instead of the ball? My carriage turned out to be a 12-year-old Dodge Ram with peeling paint and tobacco stains down the driver's side door! Instead of protecting my dainty slippers from the mud holes with his velvet cloak, Prince Charming's Ram now barrels in to the nearest Dairy Queen on date night and He says, "Well, what are you waiting for? Jump out!"

What does a girl do when she's stressed and having a bad day? She goes shopping! Ah, the mere mention of the rustling tissue paper enveloping a tulle frock can send your happiness meter soaring and salvage your long-awaited nirvana. You breeze into the nearest Macy's, hoping to clothe yourself in a newly purchased layer of chiffon, which resembles the icing on a celebration cake. After all, spring is right around the corner.

Alas, the size 6 that you made sure zipped off easily during your courtship has somehow shrunk! *Those darn designers, do they all use Victoria Beckham for their muse?* you wonder. Resigned to the fact that Cinderella cannot be seen in a size 12 (even if it feels so comfy), you must then decide shoes are the real anecdote for anxiety. *Even Victoria couldn't get by on a size zero at the Nordstroms shoe rack*, you assure yourself.

Is that rippling of your thighs from the body blows you took during the courtship?

Taking the elevator to the ground floor, you eye the latest Jimmy Choo stilettos. Surely when He sees you strutting in these babies, He will trade in the Ram for the Jag you've been wanting. You pick out a few pairs, averting your eyes from the prices marked. New shoes may be the answer, but you have serious questions as you try to pry your newly formed, webbed tennis toes into the sharp points. Have Cinderella's toes grown longer, or has the conspiracy of toppling her dynasty spread to Nordstrom corporate?

By now your feet are killing you and you're thinking maybe Spanx can solve your issues. When He sees you looking svelte in your non-forgiving size 10 and your swollen ankles swaying under the weight of your expanded torso, He will once again be blinded by the old you, right? Riiiiight. As you struggle breathlessly from fighting the body armor, you glance in the mirror and are suddenly seized with terror. Is that rippling of your thighs from the body blows you took during the courtship? Or, God forbid, does Cinderella have that much cellulite?

SILVER LININGS

Some of my musings are from personal experience. Others were shared by acquaintances. But in the end, life is a journey for all of us that holds some highs, some lows, and lots of mundane times. I know the horror of cancer. Others I know have experienced the desperation of drug abuse or an unexpected death. However, one thing we all have in common is that time moves forward if life continues.

My first 60 years were filled with drama, exhilaration and regret. It appears my journey for the next 30 years will be lived in a lovely silver lining of excitement, peace and tranquility. I am immensely grateful to my husband, Herb Weitzman, for providing my beautiful silver lining.

Our marriage added Herb's lovely daughters and their precious girls to my immediate family. It also blessed me with a cadre of interesting extended family members. Unfortunately, emotional growth isn't automatic, and I was wrong to expect instant acceptance from my new family members. At times, I have been unfair and quick to judge their motives and behaviors. Fortunately, my training as a counselor forced me to remember the value of patience, admit my mistakes, and continue my search for balanced, rational behavior. My efforts are paying off. I'm becoming the woman I want to be, and I know Herb's commitment to me, our love, and our marriage is an essential part of my journey.

ABOUT THE AUTHOR

 Donna Arp Weitzman is a wife, mother, and businesswoman who enjoys writing and a good pair of Manolo Blahniks. She and her husband live in Dallas, Texas.

Donna has been blessed by her success as a businesswoman, but nothing compares to being married and the proud mother of two Southern gentlemen, Brandon and Collin, who love their families and are successful in their own right.

She has extensive experience in the classroom and the boardroom, earning her BSE and MSE in Counseling from Midwestern State University, as well as completing the Harvard Business School OPM Management Program. Donna has served as a mayor and leader in local city government and continues to serve the greater Dallas community she loves in a variety of civic and cultural roles.

However, it's the lessons Donna has learned in the school of life that she most wants to share with others. *Cinderella Has Cellulite* is Donna's first book, and her writing has previously been published as a columnist for *The News and Times, Tri-Cities*, owned by *The Dallas Morning News*. As a frequent public speaker, she enjoys making others laugh and opening their eyes to a new perspective on some of life's most challenging experiences.

She married her husband, Herb, in 2012 and they enjoy traveling together and spending time with family and friends.